SP◉T THE DIFFERENCES

100 Challenging Photo Puzzles

STERLING

New York / London
www.sterlingpublishing.com

STERLING and the distinctive Sterling logo are registered trademarks of
Sterling Publishing Co., Inc.

Library of Congress Cataloging-in-Publication Data
Spot the differences : 100 challenging photo puzzles.
   p. cm.
   Photos from the collections of the George Eastman House.
   ISBN-13: 978-1-4027-5501-9
   ISBN-10: 1-4027-5501-5
1. Picture puzzles. 2. Visual perception. I. George Eastman House.

GV1507.P47S69 2008
793.73--dc22

                                          2007032212

                      20 19 18 17 16

            Published in 2008 by Sterling Publishing Co., Inc.
            387 Park Avenue South, New York, NY 10016

                  © 2008 by George Eastman House

            Distributed in Canada by Sterling Publishing
         c/o Canadian Manda Group, 165 Dufferin Street
              Toronto, Ontario, Canada M6K 3H6
      Distributed in the United Kingdom by GMC Distribution Services
   Castle Place, 166 High Street, Lewes, East Sussex, England BN7 1XU
      Distributed in Australia by Capricorn Link (Australia) Pty. Ltd.
            P.O. Box 704, Windsor, NSW 2756, Australia

                        Printed in China
                  Photo Alteration by Rick Schwab
               Production & layout: Oxygen Design

            Sterling ISBN-13: 978-1-4027-5501-9
                  ISBN-10: 1-4027-5501-5

   For information about custom editions, special sales, premium and
         corporate purchases, please contact Sterling Special Sales
   Department at 800-805-5489 or specialsales@sterlingpublishing.com.

Table of Contents

Introduction

Do you have a sharp eye? The pairs of pictures in this book may appear to be exactly the same—but they're not! Do you notice anything different? Is something missing? Is there something there that wasn't before? Look closely and see if you can "Spot the Differences."

Puzzles are categorized into three levels of difficulty: easy, medium, and hard. There are five differences to "spot" in the easy section, six in the medium section, and seven in the hard section. We have added colored borders around all of the original untouched pictures so you can easily distinguish them from the altered ones which have a simple cream border throughout. The originals in the easy section have green borders, in the medium section they have purple borders, and in the hard section they have orange borders. Answers appear at the back of the book.

All of the images are from the incredible George Eastman House collection, so you'll notice that many of them are well-known photos taken by acclaimed photographers—which will make the puzzle solving all the more exciting!

Good Luck!

Easy

Answer on page 109

6

Answer on page 114

Answer on page 119

8

Answer on page 124

9

Answer on page 129

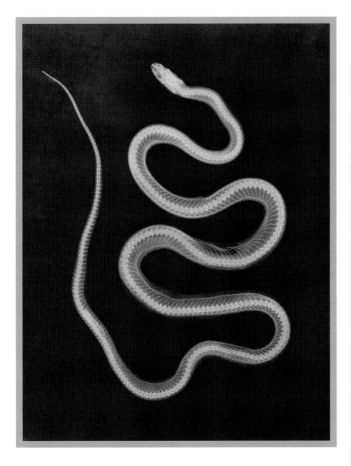

Answer on page 134

Answer on page 139

Answer on page 144

Answer on page 149

Answer on page 136

15

Answer on page 109

16

Answer on page 115

Answer on page 120

18

Answer on page 125

Answer on page 130

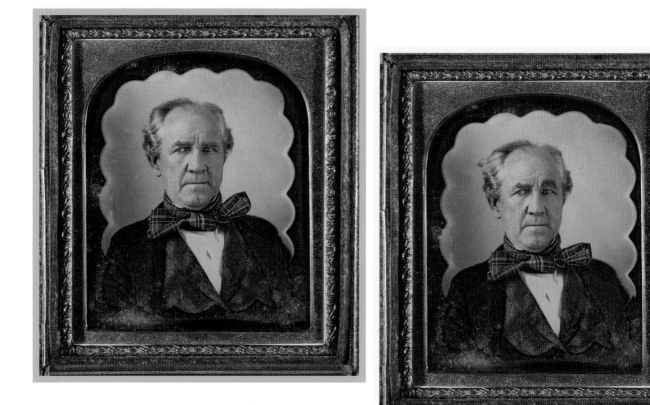

Answer on page 134

Answer on page 140

Answer on page 145

Answer on page 149

Answer on page 152

Answer on page 110

Answer on page 115

27

Answer on page 120

28

"Sitting Bull" Sioux Chief

"Sitting Bull" Sioux Chief

Answer on page 125

Answer on page 130

Answer on page 135

Answer on page 140

Answer on page 145

Answer on page 150

Answer on page 158

35

First Platinotye print made in America by William Willis jr, inventor, in 1877.

Answer on page 110

First Platinotye print made in America by William Willis jr, inventor, in 1877.

Medium

Answer on page 116

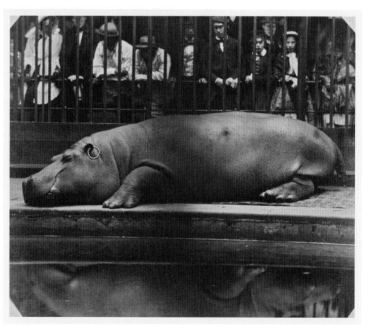

Answer on page 126

Answer on page 135

Answer on page 121

Answer on page 141

Answer on page 146

Answer on page 151

Answer on page 155

Answer on page 111

Answer on page 116

Answer on page 121

Answer on page 126

Answer on page 131

Answer on page 137

Answer on page 142

Answer on page 154

53

Answer on page 150

54

Answer on page 154

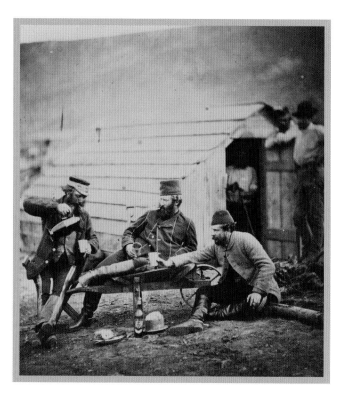

Answer on page 111

Answer on page 117

Answer on page 122

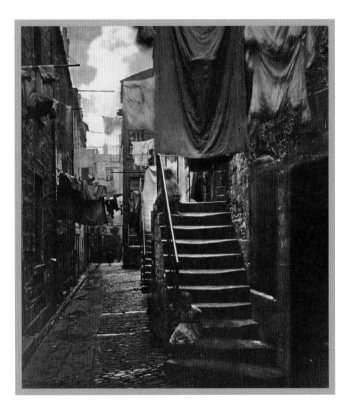

Answer on page 127

Answer on page 131

Answer on page 137

Answer on page 142

Answer on page 146

Answer on page 151

Answer on page 156

65

Answer on page 112

Answer on page 117

Answer on page 122

Answer on page 118

69

Answer on page 132

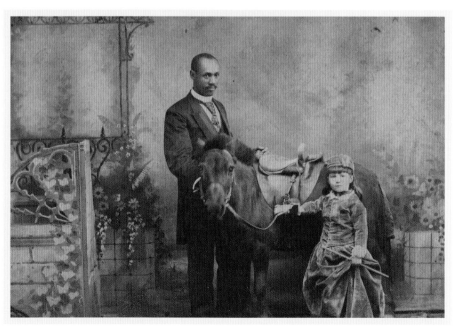

Answer on page 136

Answer on page 141

Hard

Answer on page 147

Answer on page 156

Answer on page 112

Answer on page 127

Answer on page 123

Answer on page 128

Answer on page 132

Answer on page 138

Answer on page 143

Answer on page 147

Answer on page 152

Answer on page 155

Answer on page 113

Answer on page 118

Answer on page 123

Answer on page 128

89

Answer on page 133

Answer on page 138

Answer on page 143

Answer on page 148

Answer on page 153

Answer on page 157

Answer on page 113

Answer on page 119

97

Indian "Pow-Wow" at Moosomin. N.W.T. 17ᵗʰ June 1889.

Answer on page 124

Indian "Pow-Wow" at Moosomin. N.W.T. 17ᵗʰ June 1889.

Answer on page 129

Answer on page 133

Answer on page 139

Answer on page 144

Answer on page 148

Answer on page 153

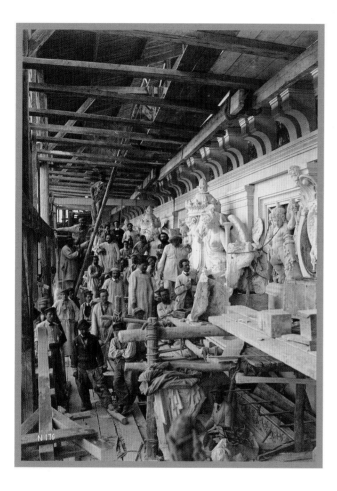

Answer on page 157

Answer on page 114

Answer on page 158

Puzzle page 16

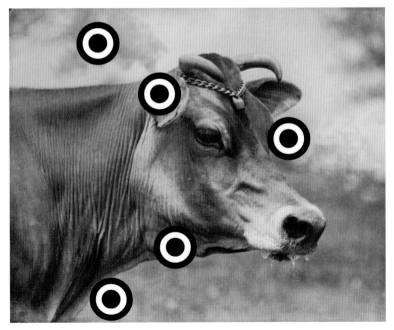

Puzzle page 6

Puzzle page 26

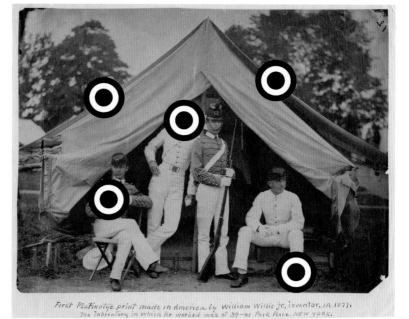

Puzzle page 36

First Platinotype print made in America by William Willis jr, inventor, in 1877. The laboratory in which he worked was at 39–41 Park Place, NEW YORK.

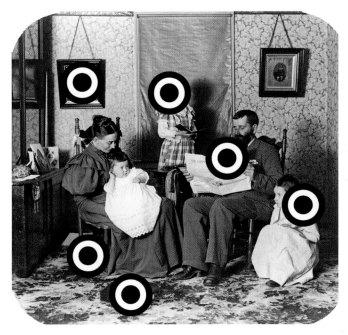

Puzzle page 46

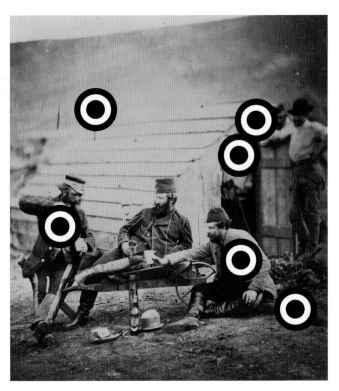

Puzzle page 56

Puzzle page 66

Puzzle page 76

Puzzle page 86

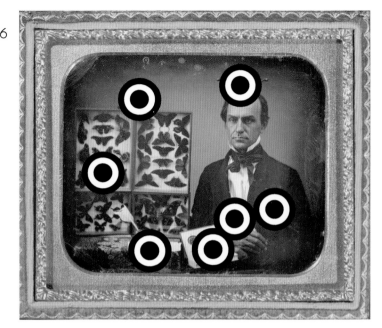

Puzzle page 96

Puzzle page 106

Puzzle page 7

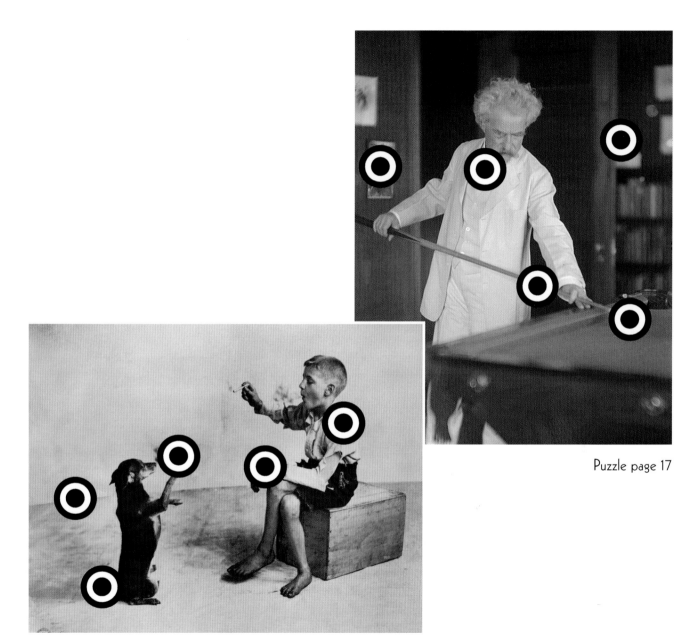

Puzzle page 17

Puzzle page 27

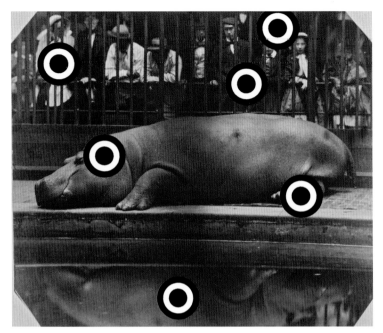

Puzzle page 38

Puzzle page 47

Puzzle page 57

Puzzle page 67

Puzzle page 69

Puzzle page 87

Puzzle page 97

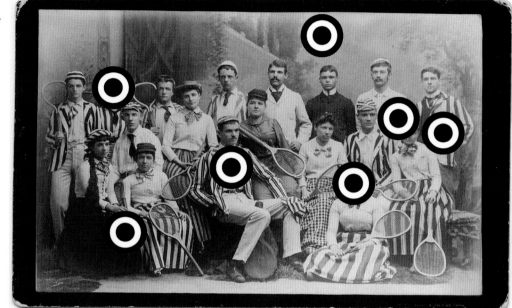

Puzzle page 8

Puzzle page 28

Puzzle page 18

Puzzle page 41

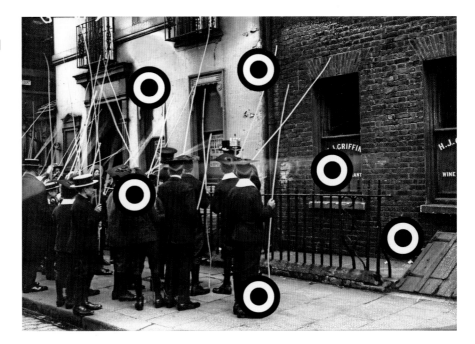

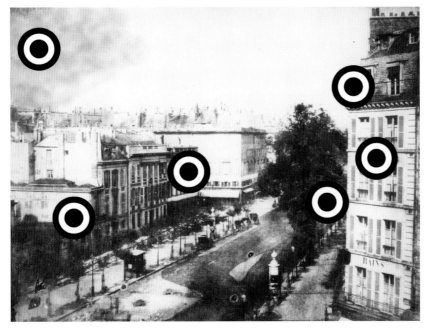

Puzzle page 48

Puzzle page 58

Puzzle page 68

122

Puzzle page 78

Puzzle page 88

Indian "Pow-Wow" at Moosomin. N.W.T. 17th June 1889.

Puzzle page 98

Puzzle page 9

124

"Sitting Bull" / Sioux Chief

Puzzle page 19

Puzzle page 39

Puzzle page 49

Puzzle page 59

Puzzle page 77

127

Puzzle page 79

Puzzle page 89

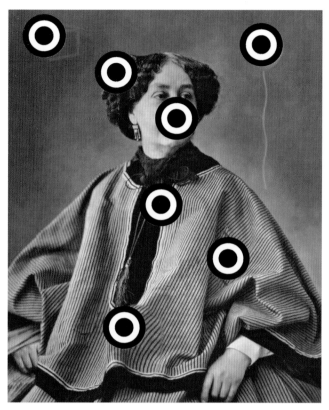

Puzzle page 99

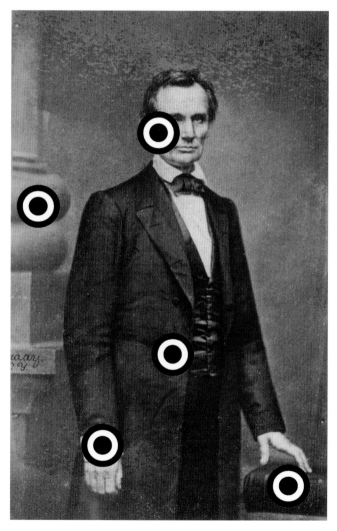

Puzzle page 10

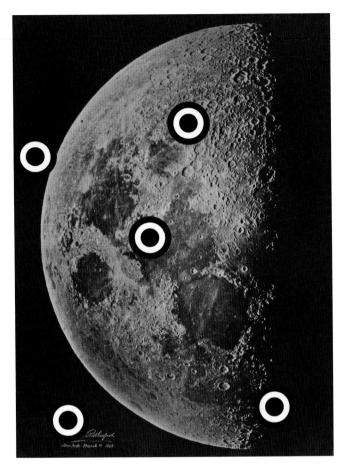

Puzzle page 20

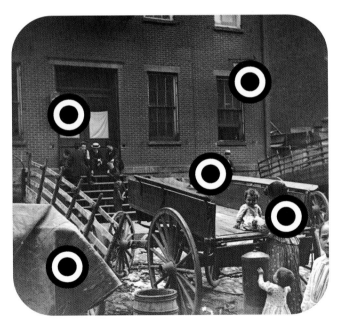

Puzzle page 30

Puzzle page 50

Puzzle page 60

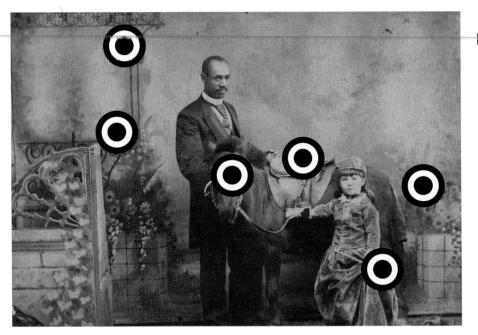

Puzzle page 70

Puzzle page 80

Puzzle page 90

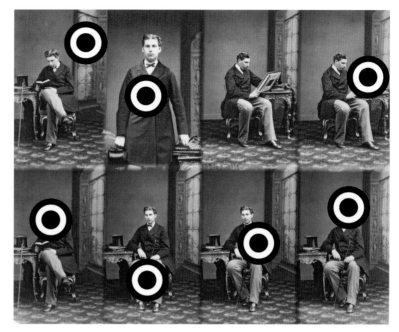

Puzzle page 100

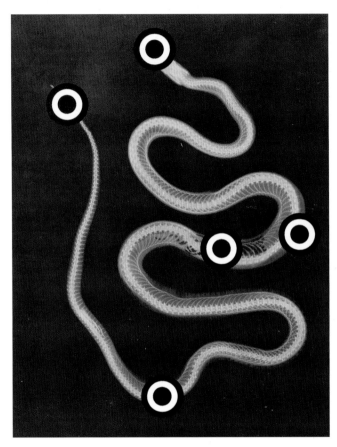

Puzzle page 11

Puzzle page 21

Puzzle page 40

Puzzle page 31

Puzzle page 15

Puzzle page 71

Puzzle page 61

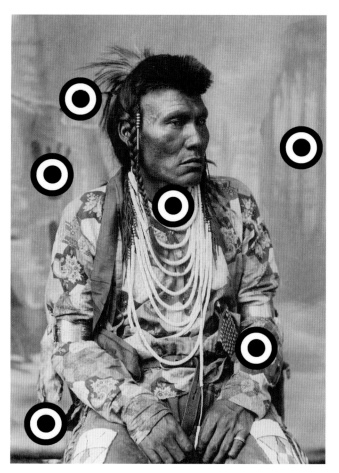

Puzzle page 51

Puzzle page 91

Puzzle page 81

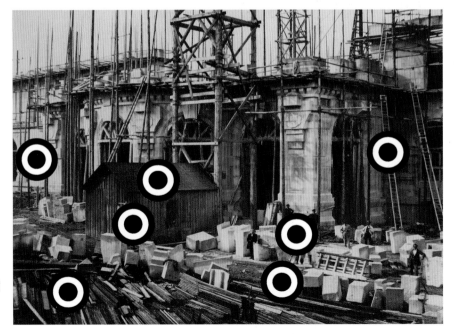

Puzzle page 101

Fresko Shutter
Same Person 4 times

Puzzle page 12

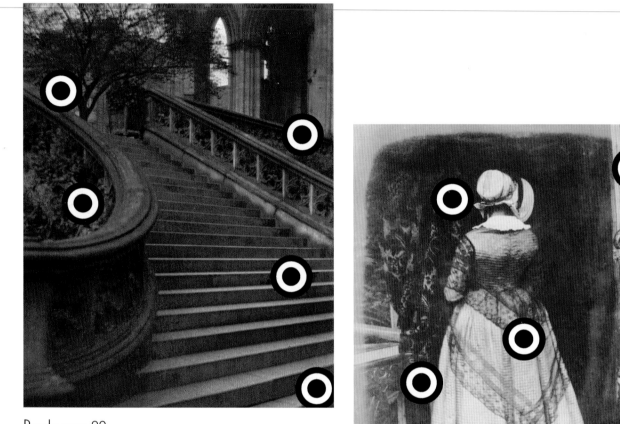

Puzzle page 22

Puzzle page 32

Puzzle page 42

Puzzle page 72

Puzzle page 52

Puzzle page 62

Puzzle page 82

Puzzle page 92

Puzzle page 102

Puzzle page 13

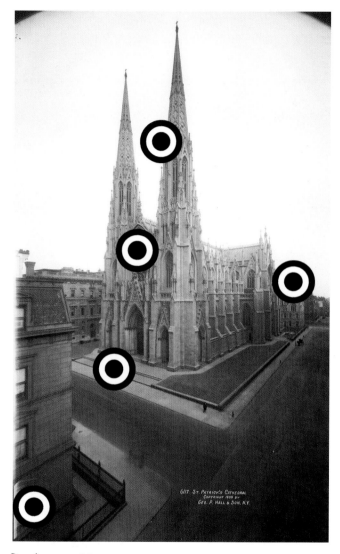

Puzzle page 33

Puzzle page 23

145

Puzzle page 43

Puzzle page 63

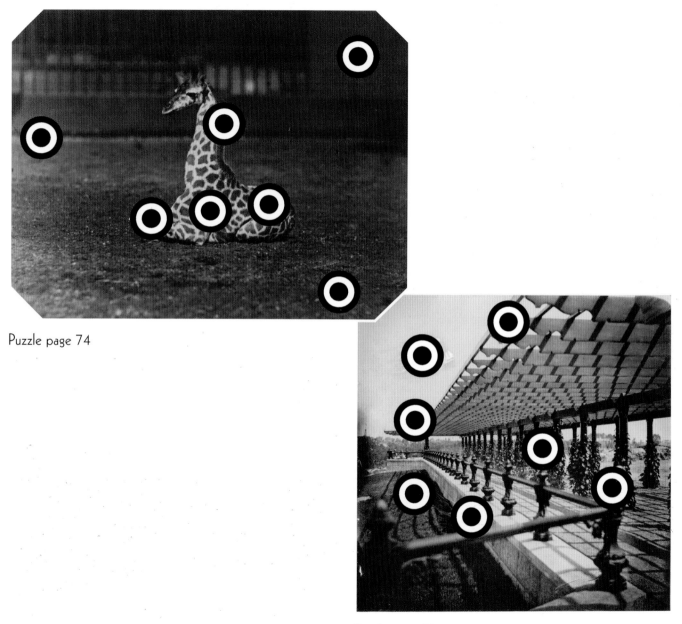

Puzzle page 74

Puzzle page 83

Puzzle page 93

Puzzle page 103

Puzzle page 24

Puzzle page 14

Puzzle page 34

Puzzle page 54

Puzzle page 44

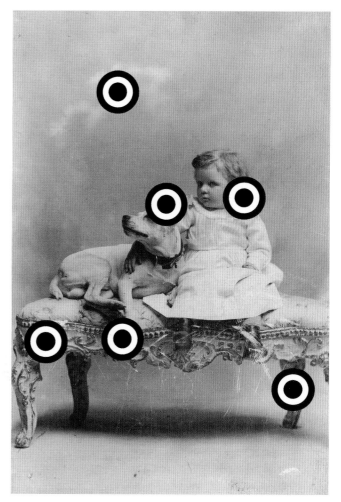

Puzzle page 64

Puzzle page 84

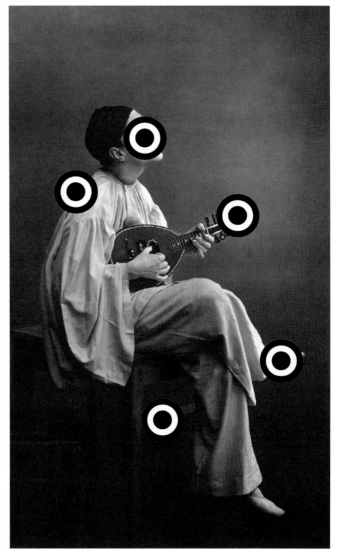

Puzzle page 25

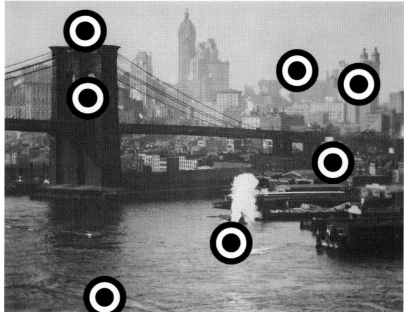

Puzzle page 94

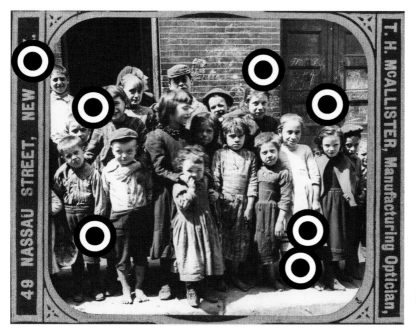

Puzzle page 104

Puzzle page 53

Puzzle page 55

Puzzle page 45

Puzzle page 85

Puzzle page 75

Puzzle page 95

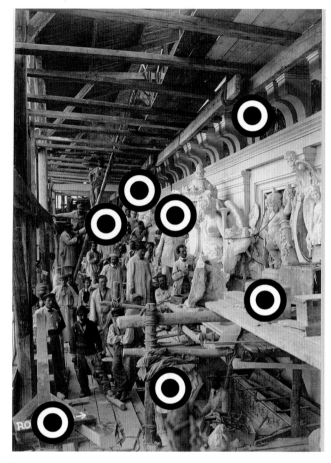

Puzzle page 105

Puzzle page 35

Puzzle page 107

Photo credits

All photos are Courtesy of the George Eastman House collection, Rochester, NY.

Page 1: Dorothea Lange (left), Lewis W. Hine (right); **Page 3:** Nathan Lazarnick (far left), Eadweard J. Muybridge, Charles C. Zoller, Count de Montizon (far right); **Page 6:** Schrieber & Sons; **Page 7:** William M. Vander Weyde; **Page 8:** Eugène Atget; **Page 9:** Edouard Baldus; **Page 10:** Mathew Brady; **Page 11:** Eduard Valenta and Dr. Josef Maria Eder; **Page 12:** T.H. McAllister; **Page 13:** Louis Jules Duboscq-Soleil; **Page 14:** Eugène Atget; **Page 15:** Èdward S. Curtis; **Page 16:** F. Jay Haynes; **Page 17:** Alvin Langdon Coburn; **Page 18:** Eugène Atget; **Page 19:** Unidentified; **Page 20:** Lewis M. Rutherfurd; **Page 21:** Unidentified; **Page 22:** Alvin Langdon Coburn; **Page 23:** Unidentified; **Page 24:** William Henry Jackson; **Page 25:** Gabriel Cromer; **Page 26:** T.H. McAllister; **Page 27:** Fitz W. Guerin; **Page 28:** Timothy H. O'Sullivan; **Page 29:** Unidentified; **Page 30:** T.H. McAllister; **Page 31:** Henri Le Secq; **Page 32:** Hill & Adamson; **Page 33:** George P. Hall & Son; **Page 34:** William M. Vander Weyde; **Page 35:** Henry Peach Robinson; **Page 36:** Pach Bros; **Page 38:** Count de Montizon; **Page 39:** Alvin Langdon Coburn; **Page 40:** Dorothea Lange; **Page 41:** Ch. Chusseau-Flaviens; **Page 42:** S. Fisher Corlies; **Page 43:** Alvin Langdon Coburn; **Page 44:** Lewis W. Hine; **Page 45:** Eugène Atget; **Page 46:** T.H. McAllister; **Page 47:** Timothy H. O'Sullivan; **Page 48:** William Henry Fox Talbot; **Page 49:** Julia Margaret Cameron; **Page 50:** Mathew Brady; **Page 51:** Boorne & May; **Page 52:** Lewis W. Hine; **Page 53:** Lewis W. Hine; **Page 54:** Charles C. Zoller; **Page 55:** Harold Corsini; **Page 56:** Roger Fenton; **Page 57:** Alvin Langdon Coburn; **Page 58:** Robert Cornelius; **Page 59:** Thomas Annan; **Page 60:** Alvin Langdon Coburn; **Page 61:** George P. Hall & Son; **Page 62:** Lewis Carroll; **Page 63:** Frantisek Fridrich; **Page 64:** Vail Bros.; **Page 65:** George P. Hall & Son; **Page 66:** Gabrielle Cromer; **Page 67:** George P. Hall & Son; **Page 68:** Hill & Adamson; **Page 69:** G.R. Fardon; **Page 70:** Charles Eisenmann; **Page 71:** Unidentified; **Page 72:** Nathan Lazarnick; **Page 74:** Count de Montizon; **Page 75:** André Giroux; **Page 76:** Frederick F. Church; **Page 77:** Delmaet & Durandelle; **Page 78:** Charles C. Zoller; **Page 79:** Timothy H. O'Sullivan; **Page 80:** William M. Grundy; **Page 81:** Delmaet & Durandelle; **Page 82:** Southworth & Hawes; **Page 83:** Victor Prevost; **Page 84:** Lewis W. Hine; **Page 85:** George Read; **Page 86:** Unidentified; **Page 87:** Eadweard J. Muybridge; **Page 88:** Hill & Adamson; **Page 89:** George P. Hall & Son; **Page 90:** André-Adolph-Eugène Disidéri; **Page 91:** George P. Hall & Son; **Page 92:** Eugène Atget; **Page 93:** Unidentified; **Page 94:** Alvin Langdon Coburn; **Page 95:** Unidentified; **Page 96:** Delmaet & Durandelle; **Page 97:** Unidentified; **Page 98:** Unidentified; **Page 99:** Nadar; **Page 100:** Robert Howlett; **Page 101:** Unidentified; **Page 102:** Isaiah West Taber; **Page 103:** Mathew Brady; **Page 104:** T.H. McAllister; **Page 105:** Delmaet & Durandelle; **Page 106:** Hill & Adamson; **Page 107:** Lewis W. Hine.